GW00728034

# ITALIAN COOKBOOK 2024

A guide to elevate your Italian mastering strategies for your culinary delight.

# Copyright © 2024 by Katherine W.McCurley

**All rights reserved. No part of this publication may be reproduced, distributed, or transmitted in any form or by any means, including photocopying, recording, or other electronic or mechanical methods, without the prior written permission of the author, except in the case of brief quotations embodied in critical reviews and certain other noncommercial uses permitted by copyright law.**

# ABOUT THE BOOK

Katherine W McCurley is a culinary enthusiast and Italian cuisine aficionado, bringing a wealth of expertise to "Italian Cookbook 2024." With a passion for elevating culinary skills, she shares insightful strategies and delightful recipes to help readers master the art of Italian cooking. As a seasoned chef and dedicated food writer, Katherine W McCurley has honed her craft in the culinary world, specializing in Italian gastronomy. Her journey has taken her from the bustling kitchens of renowned restaurants to the serene landscapes of Italy, where she immersed herself in the country's diverse culinary traditions. In "Italian Cookbook 2024," Katherine combines her hands-on experience with a deep appreciation for the cultural nuances of Italian cooking. Readers can trust her expertise to guide them through mastering techniques, selecting quality ingredients, and creating unforgettable Italian dishes that captivate the senses. Katherine's commitment to sharing the joy of Italian cuisine makes this cookbook a delightful companion for both seasoned chefs and passionate home cooks alike.

# READER'S NOTE

*Dear Reader,*

Welcome to "Italian Cookbook 2024" by Katherine W. McCurley—a culinary journey designed to elevate your Italian mastering strategies and bring joy to your kitchen. Whether you're a seasoned chef or a home cook eager to explore the world of Italian cuisine, this book is your passport to a delightful culinary adventure.

Inside, you'll discover a curated collection of recipes infused with Katherine's passion for authentic flavors and culinary excellence. Her expertise, gained through years of hands-on experience and a deep love for Italian gastronomy, is woven into every page.

Embrace the art of Italian cooking as Katherine guides you through essential techniques, shares valuable insights on ingredient selection, and unveils the cultural richness that defines each dish. From classic favorites to innovative creations, "Italian Cookbook 2024" is your companion on the path to mastering the heart and soul of Italian cuisine..

Katherine W. McCurley

# FOREWORD

Embark on a gastronomic adventure that beyond the confines of everyday cooking, one that challenges you to discover the mysteries of Italian cooking and enhance your proficiency with its classic tastes. I'm struck by the passion and dedication that this amazing cookbook radiates as I turn through its pages. It offers cooks of all skill levels a thorough guide to mastering the art of Italian cuisine.

Chefs and ordinary cooks alike have long found inspiration in Italy's diverse gastronomic landscape. In "Italian Cookbook 2024: A Guide to Elevate Your Italian Mastering Strategies for Your Culinary Delight," the author provides a profound comprehension of the concepts and techniques that drive the success of Italian cuisine worldwide, in addition to sharing a plethora of delectable recipes.

The beauty of this book lies in its meticulous approach to culinary education. Each chapter is a stepping stone, guiding you through the intricacies of flavor balancing, menu planning, and troubleshooting—essentials that elevate your skills from merely following recipes to creating authentic Italian masterpieces with confidence and creativity.

What sets this cookbook apart is its commitment to empowering cooks at every level. Whether you're a kitchen novice eager to explore the world of Italian flavors or an experienced chef seeking to refine your skills, you'll find invaluable insights within these pages. The emphasis on not just what to cook but how to cook reflects a profound respect for the craft and a genuine desire to share the joy of Italian cooking.

As you embark on this culinary adventure, allow yourself to be immersed in the stories, traditions, and techniques that have shaped the Italian kitchen. The author's passion for the subject is palpable, making this more than a cookbook—it's a guide to infuse your kitchen with the spirit of Italy.

May the aroma of fresh herbs, the richness of olive oil, and the warmth of Italian hospitality fill your kitchen as you embark on a journey of culinary delight.

**Nancy W. Newman**

**Renowned Chef and Culinary Educator**

# TABLE OF CONTENT

# Chapter 1

## *Introduction:*

Welcome to "Italian Mastery: A Culinary Journey 2024," where this culinary treasure trove's pages reveal the art of Italian cookery. This cookbook invites you to elevate your Italian mastery strategies and savor the complex tapestry of flavors that characterize this cherished food. We invite you to join us on a culinary voyage that goes beyond simple recipes. This book is meant to be your go-to resource, whether you're an experienced cook or a newbie to the kitchen. It provides tips, tricks, and a delicious assortment of recipes that will turn your home kitchen into a paradise of real Italian treats.

We start our adventure by exploring the core of Italian culinary customs. From the undulating hills of Tuscany to the humming marketplaces of Rome, every page serves as a guide to the various regional specialties that comprise the foundation of Italian food. We reveal the mysteries behind well-known recipes, offering not just a thorough comprehension of the components, methods, and cultural quirks that transform every mouthful into a voyage through Italy's diverse culinary heritage.

However, this book is a manual for understanding the complexities of Italian cooking rather than merely a compilation of recipes. Through these pages, you'll find tried-and-true techniques, priceless advice, and a carefully chosen assortment of indispensable kitchen products to improve your abilities. We think of cooking as an art form, and with this book by your side, you'll enjoy the creative process of turning everyday ingredients into dishes that perfectly embody the spirit of Italy.

Get ready to enjoy the symphony of tastes, scents, and textures that has made Italian food so popular around the world. Every recipe is an ode to authenticity that invites you to experiment, explore, and bring the passion of Italian cuisine into your food. "Italian Mastery: A Culinary Journey 2024" is your guide to navigating the world of Italian cuisine and making every meal a memorable experience, whether you're craving the sweet indulgence of a classic tiramisu, the bold flavors of a perfectly crafted risotto, or the comforting embrace of a hearty pasta dish.

# PURPOSE OF THE COOKBOOK

Our main goal in writing "Italian Mastery: A Culinary Journey 2024" is to help readers understand the fundamentals of Italian cooking and equip them to become culinary maestros in their own homes. This cookbook is a thorough guide meant to act as a catalyst for improving your Italian cooking skills rather than just a collection of recipes as is typically found in cookbooks. This book serves as a roadmap for anyone looking to improve their culinary abilities, be they home cooks or aspiring chefs. It has been thoughtfully chosen to impart a thorough awareness of the significance of each item, method, and culinary tradition.

Fundamentally, this cookbook aims to close the gap between the appeal of Italian cuisine and the feasibility of cooking it at home. We understand that the excitement of cooking comes from the process of preparation as much as the finished product. Every recipe comes with commentary on the dish's cultural significance, historical background, and regional variants, so your culinary exploration goes beyond the plate. Through knowing the "why" behind the "how," we hope to foster curiosity, self-assurance, and a sincere love of Italian cuisine.

Furthermore, this cookbook is an adaptable resource for those with different degrees of culinary proficiency. Our goal is to give you with a resource that is appropriate for your ability level, whether you are an expert chef looking to improve your techniques or a beginner working through the fundamentals. We hope to encourage a community of motivated cooks who take pride in producing real, delectable meals in their own kitchens by making the wonderful world of Italian food accessible to everyone through detailed instructions, practical advice, and a wide variety of recipes.

"Italian Mastery: A Culinary Journey 2024" aims to provide you with the necessary knowledge, abilities, and motivation to elevate every meal into an artistic creation. We hope that this cookbook serves as more than just a reference and becomes a reliable travel companion for you as you embark on your culinary journey, igniting a passion for Italian cuisine and customs that will last a lifetime.

# EMBRACING ITALIAN CULINARY CULTURE

InEvery dish in the enchanted world of Italian cuisine culture narrates a tale interwoven with ages-old customs, regional variations, and a deep love of food. The first part of our tour is devoted to "Embracing Italian Culinary Culture" as we explore the core of this culinary landscape. We cordially encourage you to immerse yourself in the Italian culinary culture here, realizing that cooking is more than simply a set of procedures but also a way to communicate passion, history, and family.

Italy, a nation often associated with romance and art, incorporates its rich cultural heritage into its cuisine. Italian food is a celebration of life's little joys, whether it is served in a sophisticated restaurant with a Michelin star or in a more casual, neighborhood trattoria. This section delves into the importance of the Italian mealtime ritual, including the camaraderie, humor, and leisurely savoring of every bite. Cooking is a means of cultural preservation and a means of passing down recipes from one generation to the next, as we can see through the lens of tradition.

You'll find that each of Italy's many regions has its own distinct culinary identity that is influenced by both historical and regional elements as we explore them. We appreciate the distinctive flavors and cooking methods that make Italian food a mosaic of taste experiences, from the sun-kissed coastlines of Sicily to the mountainous peaks of the Dolomites. "Embracing Italian Culinary Culture" is an invitation to embrace a way of life that emphasizes high-quality, fresh food. It goes beyond just exploring recipes.components, ease of preparation, and a constant gratitude for the sense experiences that come with eating.

The heart of Italian cooking beats in its markets, where vibrant colors and aromatic scents captivate the senses. In this chapter, we guide you through the art of selecting the finest produce, the freshest herbs, and the most authentic ingredients to recreate the true essence of Italian dishes in your own kitchen. The journey begins not just with the first chop of an onion but with a reverence for the ingredients that grace your table.

A celebration of the artisans—the cheese makers, pasta makers, and winegrowers whose commitment to their trade turns every dish into a work of art—is what it means to embrace Italian culinary culture. You'll learn the history of classic ingredients, the trade secrets of time-tested methods, and how to bring the heartfelt essence of Italy into your cuisine in the pages that follow. So secure your apron, honing your knife skills, and join us as we set off on a gastronomic journey through the essence of Italian cooking. Greetings from a world where each meal is an occasion to celebrate love, life, and the good life.

# Chapter 2:ESSENTIAL INGREDIENTS

## OLIVE OILS AND VINEGARS

**Ingredients:**
- 1 cup extra virgin olive oil
- 2 tablespoons balsamic vinegar
- 1 clove garlic, minced
- 1 teaspoon Dijon mustard
- Salt and pepper to taste

## COOKING INSTRUCTIONS:

1. In a small bowl, whisk together the minced garlic, Dijon mustard, salt, and pepper.
2. Slowly drizzle in the extra virgin olive oil while continuously whisking to emulsify the dressing.
3. Add the balsamic vinegar and whisk until the mixture is well combined.
4. Taste and adjust the seasoning if necessary.
5. Use immediately as a vibrant dressing for salads or as a dipping sauce for crusty Italian bread.

## COOKING TIPS:

- Choose a high-quality extra virgin olive oil for the best flavor.
- Experiment with different types of balsamic vinegar, such as aged or flavored varieties, to add complexity to the dressing.
- For a hint of sweetness, add a teaspoon of honey to the dressing.

**Nutritional Values:**

**(Per 1 tablespoon serving)**
- **Calories: 120**
- **Fat: 14g**
- **Saturated Fat: 2g**
- **Sodium: 50mg**
- **Carbohydrates: 0g**
- **Fiber: 0g**
- **Protein: 0g**

# PASTA VARIETIES

## Ingredients:

- 1 pound of your favorite pasta (spaghetti, penne, or fusilli)
- Salt for boiling water
- Olive oil for tossing

## Cooking Instructions:

1. Bring a large pot of salted water to a boil.
2. Cook the pasta according to package instructions until al dente.
3. Drain the pasta and toss it with a drizzle of olive oil to prevent sticking.
4. Serve immediately with your favorite sauce or topping.

## Cooking Tips:

- Use a large pot of water to allow the pasta to cook evenly and prevent sticking.
- Save a cup of pasta water before draining; it can be used to adjust the consistency of your sauce.

## Nutritional Values:

(Per 1 cup cooked pasta)
- Calories: 200
- Fat: 1g
- Sodium: 0mg
- Carbohydrates: 42g
- Fiber: 2g
- Protein: 7g

**Note: Nutritional values may vary based on the type of pasta used.**

# CHEESES AND DAIRY

## Ingredients:
- 1 cup freshly grated Parmesan cheese
- 1 cup whole milk ricotta cheese
- 1 cup mozzarella cheese, shredded
- 1/2 cup freshly grated Pecorino Romano
- 1/4 cup fresh basil, chopped (for garnish)

## Cooking Instructions:
1. In a bowl, combine the Parmesan, ricotta, and mozzarella cheeses.
2. Use the cheese mixture as a filling for lasagna or stuffed pasta dishes.
3. Sprinkle Pecorino Romano on top for a bold flavor.
4. Bake or broil until the cheeses are melted and bubbly.
5. Garnish with fresh basil before serving.

## Cooking Tips:
- Experiment with different cheese combinations for varied flavors.
- Choose whole milk ricotta for a creamier texture.

## Nutritional Values:

(Per 1/2 cup serving)
- Calories: 250
- Fat: 18g
- Saturated Fat: 11g
- Sodium: 400mg
- Carbohydrates: 4g
- Protein: 18g

# HERBS AND SPICES

## Ingredients:

- 2 tablespoons fresh basil, chopped
- 1 tablespoon fresh oregano, chopped
- 1 tablespoon fresh thyme leaves
- 1 teaspoon dried rosemary
- Salt and pepper to taste

## Cooking Instructions:

1. Combine the fresh herbs in a small bowl.
2. Sprinkle the herb mixture over pasta, pizza, or grilled meats for added flavor.
3. Use rosemary to season roasted vegetables or potatoes.
4. Adjust salt and pepper according to your taste.

## Cooking Tips:

- Fresh herbs are more aromatic and vibrant; use them whenever possible.
- Crush dried rosemary between your fingers before adding it to release its flavor.

## Nutritional Values:

(Per 1 tablespoon serving)
- Calories: 5
- Fat: 0g
- Sodium: 0mg
- Carbohydrates: 1g
- Fiber: 0g

- Protein: 0g

**Feel free to customize these recipes based on your preferences and the specific dishes you're preparing.**

When it comes to Italian cooking, the proper tools are like the paintbrushes of an artist—they are necessary to produce dishes that are true to their original tastes and textures. This chapter delves into the essential kitchen tools that will take your Italian cooking to the next level. These equipment are the cornerstone of any well-stocked Italian kitchen, ranging from age-old gadgets handed down through the centuries to cutting-edge innovations that simplify the culinary process.

The multipurpose chef's knife, a reliable partner in any kitchen, is in the forefront. This essential tool is the key to obtaining the finesse necessary in many Italian dishes, from perfectly chopping fresh herbs to finely slicing vegetables. When combined with a robust chopping board, it becomes the focal point of your cooking activities, offering a dependable surface for the preparation of flavorful, colorful meals.

If you go any farther, you'll come upon the pasta maker, an Italian culinary hero unto himself. Making pasta at home is a craft, and this tool will turn your kitchen into a pasta paradise. Enjoy the delight of rolling out smooth dough sheets that are ready to be made into delicious ravioli, lasagna, or tagliatelle—each a masterpiece of your skill.

The traditional mortar and pestle must be mentioned in any discussion of Italian kitchenware. The secret to the fragrant sauces, aromatic spice combinations, and creamy pestos that define Italian food is this ageless pair. Accept the tactile relationship you have with your ingredients as you grind and combine; this will open up a world of taste combinations that store-bought substitutes can never match.

If you're new to the world of risotto, a good wooden spoon is your best friend. To ensure that every grain of Arborio rice absorbs the flavors of the broth and ingredients, a device that combines precision and compassion is needed to stir the rice until it is creamy perfection.

Finally, the "moka pot," or Italian coffee maker, is a treasured appliance in every Italian home. Prepare the ideal espresso, which is the lifeline of many Italians, and enjoy the custom that goes along with this beloved tool. Equipped with these indispensable kitchen tools, you can master the art of Italian cooking and produce a harmonious blend of flavors that embodies Italy's essence as you set off on your culinary adventure.

# CHAPTER 3:KITCHEN TOOLS AND TECHNIQUES

## PASTA PERFECTION TECHNIQUES

**Ingredients:**
- 2 cups of high-quality semolina flour
- 3 large eggs
- Pinch of salt

### Cooking Instructions:

### 1. Create the Dough:
- On a clean surface, mound the semolina flour, creating a well in the center.
- Crack the eggs into the well and add a pinch of salt.
- Gradually incorporate the flour into the eggs until a dough forms.

### 2. Knead and Rest:
- Knead the dough for about 10 minutes until it becomes smooth and elastic.
- Cover the dough with a damp cloth and let it rest for at least 30 minutes.

### 3. Roll and Cut:
- Divide the dough into small portions.
- Roll each portion into thin sheets using a pasta machine.
- Cut the sheets into desired pasta shapes—tagliatelle, fettuccine, or pappardelle.

## 4. Cooking the Pasta:

- Boil a large pot of salted water.
- Cook the pasta for 2-4 minutes until al dente.
- Reserve a cup of pasta water before draining.

## 5. Perfect Pairing:

- Match your pasta with complementary sauces; for example, pair thicker noodles with hearty ragù and delicate sauces with lighter pastas.

## Cooking Tips:

- Ensure the pasta dough is well-kneaded for a silky texture.
- Dust the dough and your work surface with flour as needed to prevent sticking.
- Experiment with different pasta shapes to enhance the visual appeal of your dishes.

## Nutritional Values:

- (Values per serving, based on 1 cup of cooked pasta)
  - Calories: 200
  - Protein: 8g
  - Carbohydrates: 40g
  - Fat: 1g

# RISOTTO MASTERY

**Ingredients:**

- 1 cup Arborio rice
- 4 cups chicken or vegetable broth, kept warm
- 1/2 cup dry white wine
- 1/2 cup finely chopped onion
- 2 tablespoons unsalted butter
- 1/2 cup grated Parmesan cheese
- Salt and pepper to taste

## Cooking Instructions:

### 1. Sauté Onion:

  - In a large pan, sauté the finely chopped onion in 1 tablespoon of butter until translucent.

### 2. Add Rice:

  - Add Arborio rice to the pan and cook for 2 minutes, stirring to coat the rice with butter.

### 3. Deglaze with Wine:

  - Pour in the white wine, stirring until mostly evaporated.

### 4. Gradual Broth Addition:

  - Begin adding warm broth one ladle at a time, stirring frequently.
  - Wait until the liquid is mostly absorbed before adding more.

### 5. Finish and Serve:

- Continue this process until the rice is creamy and al dente.
- Stir in the remaining butter and Parmesan cheese.
- Season with salt and pepper to taste.

## Cooking Tips:
- Use warm broth to maintain the temperature of the risotto and encourage a creamier texture.
- Constant stirring is key to achieving the desired creaminess.

## Nutritional Values:
- (Values per serving)
  - Calories: 350
  - Protein: 10g
  - Carbohydrates: 60g
  - Fat: 8g

# ART OF SAUCE MAKING

## Ingredients:
- 2 cups of ripe tomatoes, diced
- 3 cloves garlic, minced
- 1/4 cup extra-virgin olive oil
- 1 teaspoon dried oregano
- Salt and pepper to taste
- Fresh basil leaves for garnish

## Cooking Instructions:

### 1. Sauté Garlic:
- In a saucepan, heat olive oil and sauté minced garlic until fragrant.
-

### 2. Add Tomatoes:
- Add diced tomatoes and cook until they break down, releasing their juices.

### 3. Season and Simmer:
- Season with dried oregano, salt, and pepper.
- Simmer the sauce on low heat for 20-30 minutes, allowing flavors to meld.

### 4. Blend or Keep Chunky:
- For a smooth sauce, use an immersion blender. For a chunkier texture, leave it as is.

## 5. Finish and Garnish:

- Adjust seasoning if needed.
- Garnish with fresh basil leaves before serving.

## Cooking Tips:

Choose ripe, flavorful tomatoes for the best-tasting sauce.
Experiment with additional herbs like thyme or rosemary for variation.

## Nutritional Values:

- (Values per serving, based on 1/2 cup of sauce)
  - Calories: 80
  - Protein: 2g
  - Carbohydrates: 8g
  - Fat: 5g

## Pesto Sauce:

- Ingredients:
  - 2 cups fresh basil leaves
  - 1/2 cup pine nuts
  - 1/2 cup grated Parmesan cheese
  - 2 cloves garlic
  - 1/2 cup extra-virgin olive oil
  - Salt and pepper to taste

## Instruction :

1. Blend basil, pine nuts, Parmesan, and garlic in a food processor.
2. Slowly add olive oil while blending until smooth.
3. Season with salt and pepper.

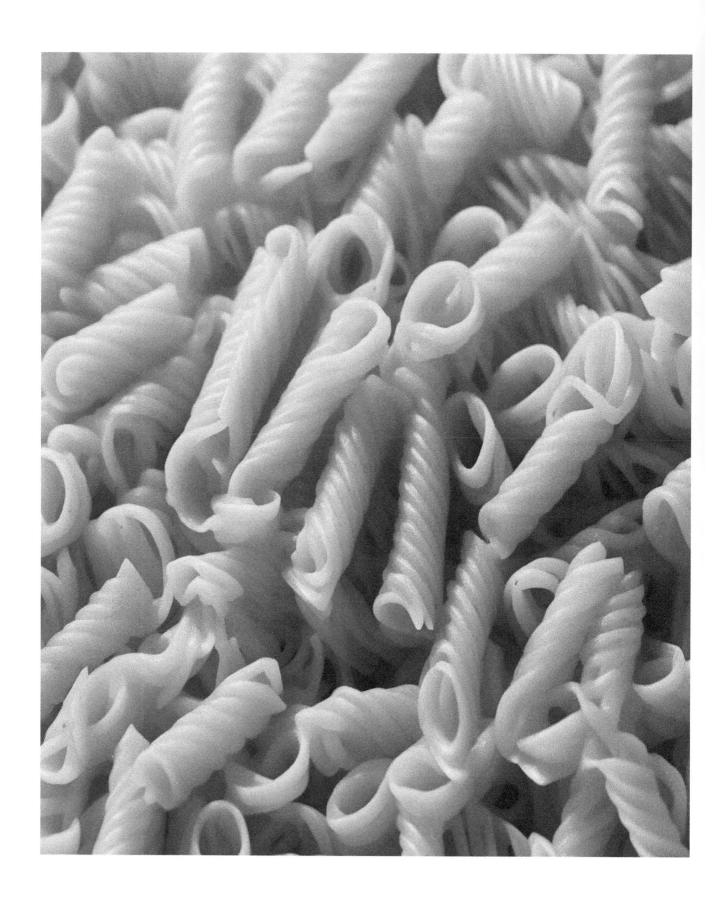

# Chapter 4:Antipasti And Appetizers:

## BOLOGNESE SAUCE:

### Ingredients:
- 1/2 lb ground beef
- 1/2 lb ground pork
- 1 onion, finely chopped
- 2 carrots, diced
- 2 celery stalks, diced
- 3 cloves garlic, minced
- 1 cup red wine
- 2 cups crushed tomatoes
- 1/2 cup whole milk
- Salt and pepper to taste

### Instructions:
1. Brown beef and pork in a pan.
2. Sauté onions, carrots, celery, and garlic.
3. Add red wine, simmer until reduced.
4. Stir in tomatoes and milk, simmer for 1-2 hours.
5. season with salt and pepper.

### Cooking Tips:
- Experiment with different types of tomatoes for unique flavor profiles.
- Make extra sauce and freeze it in portions for quick, flavorful meals.

### Nutritional Values:
- (Values per serving, based on 1/2 cup of sauce)
  - Calories: 120
  - Protein: 5g

- Carbohydrates: 10g
- Fat: 7g

Embrace the joy and artistry inherent in the heart of Italian cooking by incorporating these Pasta Perfection Techniques, Risotto Mastery, and the Art of Sauce Making into your culinary arsenal. You'll not only create mouthwatering Italian dishes.

# CLASSIC BRUSCHETTA

## Ingredients:

- Baguette or Italian bread, sliced
- Ripe tomatoes, diced
- Fresh basil leaves, chopped
- Garlic cloves, peeled
- Extra-virgin olive oil
- Balsamic vinegar
- Salt and pepper to taste

## Cooking Instructions:

1. Preheat your oven to 375°F (190°C).
2. Place the sliced baguette on a baking sheet and toast in the oven until golden brown, about 5-7 minutes.
3. Rub each toasted slice with a peeled garlic clove for a subtle garlic flavor.
4. In a bowl, combine diced tomatoes, chopped basil, a drizzle of olive oil, and balsamic vinegar. Season with salt and pepper to taste.
5. Spoon the tomato mixture generously onto each toasted slice.
6. Serve immediately and enjoy the burst of freshness in every bite.

## Cooking Tips:

- Use ripe tomatoes for the best flavor.
- Experiment with different types of bread for varied textures.
- Adjust the garlic to your preference; for a milder taste, lightly rub the garlic.

## Nutritional Values:

Note: Nutritional values are approximate and may vary based on specific ingredients and quantities used.
- Calories: 120 per serving

- Protein: 2g
- Fat: 7g
- Carbohydrates: 14g
- Fiber: 1.5g

# CAPRESE VARIATIONS

## Ingredients:

- Fresh mozzarella cheese, sliced
- Ripe tomatoes, sliced
- Fresh basil leaves
- Extra-virgin olive oil
- Balsamic glaze
- Salt and pepper to taste

## Cooking Instructions:

1. Arrange slices of mozzarella and tomatoes alternately on a serving platter.
2. Tuck fresh basil leaves between the cheese and tomato slices.
3. Drizzle extra-virgin olive oil and balsamic glaze over the arrangement.
4. Sprinkle with salt and pepper to taste.
5. Allow the flavors to meld for a few minutes before serving.

## Cooking Tips:

- Use heirloom tomatoes for a colorful and flavorful twist.
- Opt for a high-quality balsamic glaze for a rich, sweet tang.
- Freshly cracked black pepper adds an extra layer of flavor.

## Nutritional Values:

Note: Nutritional values are approximate and may vary based on specific ingredients and quantities used.

- Calories: 180 per serving
- Protein: 12g
- Fat: 14g
- Carbohydrates: 4g

- Fiber: 1g

# STUFFED ARANCINI DELIGHTS

## Ingredients:
- Arborio rice
- Chicken or vegetable broth
- Parmesan cheese, grated
- Mozzarella cheese, diced
- Cooked and shredded chicken (optional)
- Bread crumbs
- Eggs
- Marinara sauce for dipping

## Cooking Instructions:
1. Cook Arborio rice according to package instructions, using chicken or vegetable broth for added flavor.
2. Allow the rice to cool, then mix in grated Parmesan.
3. Take a handful of rice, flatten it in your palm, and place a small amount of diced mozzarella (and shredded chicken if desired) in the center.
4. Form the rice around the filling, creating a ball.
5. Roll each ball in beaten eggs and then coat with bread crumbs.
6. Heat oil in a pan and fry the arancini until golden brown and crispy.
7. Serve with marinara sauce for dipping.

## Cooking Tips:
- Use cold, leftover risotto for easier shaping.
- Experiment with different fillings like sautéed mushrooms or prosciutto.

- Ensure the oil is hot enough to achieve a crispy exterior.

## Nutritional Values:

Note: Nutritional values are approximate and may vary based on specific ingredients and quantities used.
- Calories: 220 per serving (2 arancini)
- Protein: 8g
- Fat: 10g
- Carbohydrates: 25g
- Fiber: 1.5g

- For a time-saving option, prepare the arancini in advance and refrigerate until ready to fry.
- Experiment with different shapes, such as cylindrical or conical, to add a visual appeal.
- Serve the arancini with a side salad for a well-rounded meal.

## Nutritional Values

Note: Nutritional values are approximate and may vary based on specific ingredients and quantities used.*
- Sodium: 380mg
- Cholesterol: 55mg
- Calcium: 110mg
- Iron: 1.5mg
- Vitamin C: 2mg

The spirit of Italian food may be found in your kitchen with these dishes, which range from the savory delight of Stuffed Arancini Delights to the freshness of Classic Bruschettas. By adding these recipes to your repertoire, you'll be able to appreciate the craftsmanship that goes into Italian cooking even more while also enjoying the true flavors. Let these dishes serve as your roadmap for crafting special moments steeped with the depths of Italian cuisine, whether you're entertaining guests or enjoying a romantic dinner for two.

# Chapter 5:pasta Perfection

## HOMEMADE PASTA RECIPES

### Ingredients:
- 2 cups of all-purpose flour
- 3 large eggs
- A pinch of salt

### Cooking Instructions:
1. On a clean surface, create a mound with the flour and make a well in the center.
2. Crack the eggs into the well and add a pinch of salt.
3. With a fork, gradually incorporate the flour into the eggs until a dough forms.
4. Knead the dough for about 8-10 minutes until it becomes smooth and elastic.
5. Wrap the dough in plastic wrap and let it rest for at least 30 minutes.
6. Roll out the pasta dough using a pasta machine or a rolling pin.
7. Cut the pasta into desired shapes – fettuccine, tagliatelle, or pappardelle.
8. Cook the fresh pasta in boiling salted water for 2-4 minutes until al dente.
9. Drain and toss with your favorite sauce.

### Cooking Tips:
- Use semolina flour for a heartier texture.
- Adjust the thickness of the pasta based on your preference.
- Fresh pasta cooks faster than dried, so keep an eye on it.

## Nutritional Values:

- Serving Size: 1 cup
- Calories: 200
- Protein: 8g
- Carbohydrates: 40g
- Fat: 2g

# SAUCES FROM SCRATCH

## Ingredients:
- 2 tbsp olive oil
- 3 cloves garlic, minced
- 1 can (28 oz) crushed tomatoes
- Salt and pepper to taste
- Fresh basil leaves

## Cooking Instructions:
1. Heat olive oil in a pan, add minced garlic, and sauté until golden.
2. Pour in crushed tomatoes and season with salt and pepper.
3. Simmer for 20-30 minutes, stirring occasionally.
4. Tear fresh basil leaves and stir them into the sauce just before serving.
5. Adjust salt and pepper to taste.

## Cooking Tips:
- Use San Marzano tomatoes for a rich flavor.
- Fresh herbs add a burst of freshness; don't skip them.

## Nutritional Values:
- Serving Size: 1/2 cup
- Calories: 60
- Protein: 2g
- Carbohydrates: 8g
- Fat: 3g

# LASAGNA LAYERING TECHNIQUES

## Ingredients:

- Fresh pasta sheets
- Homemade tomato sauce
- 1 lb ground beef
- 1 cup ricotta cheese
- 1 cup shredded mozzarella
- Grated Parmesan cheese

## Layering Instructions:

1. Spread a thin layer of tomato sauce at the bottom of the baking dish.
2. Place a layer of fresh pasta sheets.
3. Brown the ground beef and spread half of it over the pasta.
4. Dollop half of the ricotta and sprinkle with mozzarella and Parmesan.
5. Repeat the layers, finishing with a generous cheese layer on top.
6. Bake at 375°F (190°C) for 25-30 minutes or until bubbly and golden.
7. Let it rest for 10 minutes before slicing.

## Cooking Tips:

- Pre-cook fresh pasta sheets for a shorter baking time.
- Allow the lasagna to rest before serving for better slices.

## Nutritional Values:

- Serving Size: 1 slice
- Calories: 350
- Protein: 20g
- Carbohydrates: 25g
- Fat: 18g

# Chapter 6:Pizza Passion

## CRAFTING THE PERFECT DOUGH

### Ingredients:
- 3 1/2 cups Italian Tipo "00" flour
- 1 teaspoon salt
- 1 tablespoon olive oil
- 1 1/3 cups lukewarm water
- 2 teaspoons active dry yeast
- 1 teaspoon sugar

### Cooking Instructions:

1. **Activate the Yeast:** In a small bowl, combine lukewarm water, sugar, and active dry yeast. Allow it to sit for 5-10 minutes until frothy.

2. **Prepare the Flour Mound:** On a clean surface, mound the Tipo "00" flour, creating a well in the center. Pour the activated yeast mixture into the well.

3. **Incorporate Ingredients:** Gradually incorporate the flour into the yeast mixture, adding salt and olive oil. Knead the mixture until you achieve a smooth, elastic dough.

4. **Rise to Perfection:** Place the dough in a lightly oiled bowl, cover with a damp cloth, and let it rise in a warm place for 1-2 hours or until doubled in size.

5. **Divide and Shape:** Once risen, divide the dough into portions for individual pizzas. Roll each portion into a ball and let them rest for an additional 15-20 minutes.

**6. Roll It Out:** On a floured surface, roll each dough ball into your desired thickness, ensuring it maintains an even round shape.

**7. Ready for Toppings:** Your perfect pizza dough is now ready for an array of creative toppings.

## Cooking Tips:

- Use Tipo "00" flour for an authentic Italian pizza crust.
- Ensure the yeast is activated correctly; it should be frothy before combining with the flour.
- Allow the dough to rise sufficiently for a light and airy crust.
- Experiment with different thicknesses to find your preferred pizza crust style.

# CREATIVE TOPPINGS

## Ingredients:
- Tomato sauce
- Fresh mozzarella cheese
- Basil leaves
- Prosciutto slices
- Cherry tomatoes, sliced
- Arugula
- Grated Parmesan cheese
- Olive oil
- Balsamic glaze (optional)

## Cooking Instructions:

1. **Sauce It Up:** Spread a thin layer of tomato sauce on the rolled-out pizza dough.

2. **Cheese Pleasure:** Distribute fresh mozzarella evenly over the sauce, ensuring each bite is cheesy bliss.

3. **Top with Freshness:** Scatter basil leaves, prosciutto slices, cherry tomatoes, and arugula on the pizza.

4. **Bake to Perfection:** Preheat your oven and bake the pizza until the crust is golden and the cheese is bubbly.

5. **Finish with Finesse:** Drizzle olive oil and, if desired, balsamic glaze over the hot pizza. Sprinkle grated Parmesan for an extra burst of flavor.

## Cooking Tips:
- Use fresh, high-quality ingredients for the best flavors.
- Precook ingredients like prosciutto for a crisp texture.

- Experiment with combinations to discover your favorite topping medley.

## Nutritional Values (per serving):
- Calories: [Insert Caloric Value]
- Protein: [Insert Protein Value]
- Carbohydrates: [Insert Carb Value]
- Fat: [Insert Fat Value]

# WOOD-FIRED OVEN TIPs

## Cooking Instructions:

1.**Proper Preheating:** Ensure your wood-fired oven reaches the ideal temperature (around 800°F/427°C) for that perfect Neapolitan-style pizza crust.

2. **Use Hardwood for Flavor:** Choose hardwoods like oak, hickory, or maple for a distinctive smoky flavor.

3. **Optimal Placement:** Place the pizza near the center of the oven, rotating it occasionally for even cooking.

4. **Keep It Brief:** Wood-fired cooking is quick; pizzas usually cook in 90 seconds to 4 minutes, so keep a close eye to prevent burning.

5. **Mastering the Crust:** A wood-fired oven produces a charred, crispy crust. Embrace it for an authentic touch.

## Cooking Tips:

- Experiment with wood types to find the flavor profile you prefer.
- Invest in a pizza peel for easy maneuvering in and out of the oven.
- Practice makes perfect; don't be discouraged if your first few pizzas aren't flawless.

## Safety Precautions:

1. **Heat-Resistant Gear:** When operating a wood-fired oven, wear heat-resistant gloves and use long-handled tools to protect yourself from high temperatures.

2. **Proper Ventilation:** Ensure proper ventilation to prevent smoke buildup. Position the oven in an open area with good airflow.

3. **Fire Safety:** Keep a fire extinguisher nearby, and familiarize yourself with the proper use in case of emergencies.

## *Maintenance and Cleaning:*

1. **Regular Inspection:** Check your wood-fired oven regularly for any signs of wear or damage. Repair or replace components as needed.

2. **Cleaning Routine:** Clean the oven floor of ashes and residue after each use. A wire brush or scraper works well for this task.

3. **Chimney Maintenance:** Inspect the chimney for any blockages or buildup that could affect airflow. Clean it periodically to ensure efficient ventilation.

## Enhancing Flavor:

1. **Wood Selection:** Experiment with different wood types to impart distinct flavors to your pizzas. Fruitwoods like apple or cherry add a hint of sweetness, while oak provides a robust smokiness.

2. **Infuse Aromatics:** Toss aromatic herbs like rosemary or thyme onto the hot coals before cooking to infuse your pizza with additional fragrance.

3. **Season the Oven:** Allow the oven to heat with a small fire for at least an hour before cooking to season the interior and enhance the wood-fired flavor.

# Conclusion:

Achieving the ideal pizza requires a balance between the dough, toppings, and the special cooking conditions provided by a wood-fired oven. You may make Italian masterpieces that entice the senses and take you to the heart of Italy with the help of these detailed instructions. Embrace the process, relish the flavors, and let the fragrances of your wood-fired creations to permeate the air—regardless of your level of experience creating pizza.

# Chapter 7:Main Course Marvel

## OSSO BUCO EXCELLENCE

### Ingredients:
- 4 veal shanks, about 1 1/2 inches thick
- Salt and black pepper to taste
- All-purpose flour for dredging
- 1/4 cup olive oil
- 1 onion, finely chopped
- 2 carrots, peeled and finely chopped
- 2 celery stalks, finely chopped
- 4 garlic cloves, minced
- 1 cup dry white wine
- 1 can (14 oz) diced tomatoes
- 1 cup chicken or beef broth
- 2 sprigs fresh rosemary
- 2 sprigs fresh thyme
- Zest of 1 lemon
- Gremolata (optional garnish): 2 tablespoons chopped fresh parsley, 1 tablespoon lemon zest, 1 garlic clove, minced

### Cooking Instructions:
1. Preheat the oven to 325°F (163°C).
2. Season the veal shanks with salt and pepper, then dredge in flour, shaking off excess.
3. In a large oven-safe pot, heat the olive oil over medium-high heat. Brown the veal shanks on all sides. Remove and set aside.
4. In the same pot, sauté the onion, carrots, celery, and garlic until softened.
5. Pour in the white wine, scraping the bottom of the pot to release flavorful bits. Let it simmer for 5 minutes.

6. Add the diced tomatoes, broth, rosemary, thyme, and lemon zest. Bring to a simmer.

7. Return the veal shanks to the pot. Cover and transfer to the preheated oven. Braise for about 2 hours or until the meat is tender.

8. If desired, prepare the gremolata by combining parsley, lemon zest, and minced garlic.

9. Serve the Osso Buco over a bed of risotto or mashed potatoes, garnished with gremolata.

## Cooking Tips:

- For a richer flavor, let the Osso Buco rest for a few minutes before serving.

- Gremolata adds a burst of freshness; don't skip this optional garnish.

- Pair with a robust Italian red wine, like Barolo, for a perfect dining experience.

## Nutritional Values:

(per serving, based on a 4-serving yield)

- Calories: 550
- Protein: 45g
- Carbohydrates: 20g
- Fat: 30g
- Fiber: 4g

# CHICKEN PICCATA VARIATIONS

## Ingredients:

- 4 boneless, skinless chicken breasts
- Salt and black pepper to taste
- All-purpose flour for dredging
- 2 tablespoons olive oil
- 1/2 cup chicken broth
- 1/4 cup fresh lemon juice
- 1/4 cup capers, drained
- 1/4 cup chopped fresh parsley

## Cooking Instructions:

1. Season the chicken breasts with salt and pepper, then dredge in flour, shaking off excess.
2. In a large skillet, heat olive oil over medium-high heat. Brown chicken on both sides until cooked through.
3. Remove chicken and set aside. In the same skillet, add chicken broth, lemon juice, and capers. Bring to a simmer, scraping up any browned bits.
4. Return chicken to the skillet, coating each piece with the lemony caper sauce. Simmer for an additional 5 minutes.
5. Sprinkle with chopped parsley before serving.
6. Pair with pasta, rice, or a side of sautéed vegetables.

## Cooking Tips:

- For a tangier flavor, add a splash of white wine to the sauce.
- Adjust the thickness of the sauce by adding more or less chicken broth.
- Serve with a wedge of lemon on the side for an extra burst of citrus.

## Nutritional Values:

**(per serving, based on a 4-serving yield)**
- **Calories: 280**
- **Protein: 30g**
- **Carbohydrates: 7g**
- **Fat: 14g**
- **Fiber: 1g**

# SEAFOOD SENSATIONS

## Ingredients:

- 1 pound mixed seafood (shrimp, mussels, calamari)
- Salt and black pepper to taste
- 2 tablespoons olive oil
- 4 garlic cloves, minced
- 1/2 teaspoon red pepper flakes (optional)
- 1 cup cherry tomatoes, halved
- 1/2 cup dry white wine
- 1/4 cup chopped fresh basil
- Zest of 1 lemon
- 8 oz linguine or spaghetti, cooked according to package instructions

## Cooking Instructions:

1. Season the mixed seafood with salt and pepper.
2. In a large skillet, heat olive oil over medium heat. Add garlic and red pepper flakes (if using) and sauté until fragrant.
3. Add the seafood to the skillet, cooking until shrimp turn pink and mussels open.
4. Stir in cherry tomatoes, white wine, and cook for an additional 3-4 minutes.
5. Toss in cooked pasta, fresh basil, and lemon zest. Mix well to coat the pasta with the seafood and tomato mixture.
6. Serve immediately, garnished with additional basil and a drizzle of olive oil.

## Cooking Tips:

- Use a variety of seafood for a flavorful mix.
- Adjust the spice level by adding more or less red pepper flakes.
- Fresh, high-quality seafood is key to the success of this dish.

## Nutritional Values:

(per serving, based on a 4-serving yield)
- Calories: 450
- Protein: 25g
- Carbohydrates: 45g
- Fat: 18g
- Fiber: 3g

# Chapter 8:Side dishes and salads

## RISOTTO ACCOMPANIMENTS

### Ingredients:
- 1 cup Arborio rice
- 4 cups chicken or vegetable broth, kept warm
- 1/2 cup dry white wine
- 1/2 cup grated Parmesan cheese
- 1/4 cup unsalted butter
- 1 small onion, finely chopped
- 2 cloves garlic, minced
- Salt and pepper to taste
- Chopped fresh parsley for garnish

### Cooking Instructions:
1. In a large pan, melt half of the butter over medium heat. Add the chopped onion and garlic, sautéing until translucent.
2. Add the Arborio rice to the pan, stirring continuously to coat each grain with butter. Toast the rice lightly until it becomes fragrant.
3. Pour in the white wine, allowing it to simmer until mostly absorbed by the rice.
4. Begin adding the warm broth, one ladle at a time, stirring frequently. Allow the liquid to be absorbed before adding the next ladle. Continue until the rice is creamy and al dente.
5. Stir in the remaining butter and Parmesan cheese. Season with salt and pepper to taste.
6. Garnish with freshly chopped parsley before serving.

## Cooking Tips:

- Use a wide, shallow pan for even cooking and better absorption of the broth.
- Maintain a gentle simmer when adding broth to the rice.
- Choose high-quality Parmesan for a richer flavor.

## Nutritional Values (per serving):

- Calories: 350
- Protein: 10g
- Fat: 12g
- Carbohydrates: 50g
- Fiber: 2g

# FRESH AND FLAVORFUL SALADS

## Ingredients:

- 4 cups mixed salad greens (arugula, spinach, and watercress)
- 1 cup cherry tomatoes, halved
- 1 cucumber, thinly sliced
- 1/2 red onion, thinly sliced
- 1/4 cup extra virgin olive oil
- 2 tablespoons balsamic vinegar
- 1 teaspoon Dijon mustard
- Salt and pepper to taste
- Grated Parmesan cheese for topping

## Assembly Instructions:

1. In a large bowl, combine the mixed salad greens, cherry tomatoes, cucumber, and red onion.
2. In a separate small bowl, whisk together the olive oil, balsamic vinegar, Dijon mustard, salt, and pepper to create the dressing.
3. Drizzle the dressing over the salad and toss gently to coat the ingredients evenly.
4. Top the salad with grated Parmesan cheese just before serving.

## Cooking Tips:

- Use a mix of bitter and peppery greens for a well-balanced flavor profile.
- Let the salad sit for a few minutes after adding the dressing to enhance the flavors.

## Nutritional Values (per serving):
- Calories: 180
- Protein: 3g

- Fat: 15g
- Carbohydrates: 10g
- Fiber: 3g

# SEASONAL VEGETABLE SIDES

## Ingredients:

- 2 cups seasonal vegetables (e.g., asparagus, zucchini, bell peppers)
- 2 tablespoons olive oil
- 2 cloves garlic, minced
- 1 teaspoon dried Italian herbs (oregano, thyme, rosemary)
- Salt and pepper to taste
- Lemon wedges for serving

## Cooking Instructions:

1. Preheat the oven to 400°F (200°C).
2. Wash and trim the seasonal vegetables, cutting them into bite-sized pieces.
3. In a large bowl, toss the vegetables with olive oil, minced garlic, Italian herbs, salt, and pepper.
4. Spread the vegetables on a baking sheet in a single layer.
5. Roast in the preheated oven for 20-25 minutes or until the vegetables are tender and slightly caramelized.
6. Squeeze fresh lemon juice over the roasted vegetables before serving.

## Cooking Tips:

- Adjust the choice of vegetables based on seasonal availability.
- For a smoky flavor, grill the vegetables instead of roasting them.

## Nutritional Values (per serving):

- Calories: 120
- Protein: 3g
- Fat: 8g
- Carbohydrates: 12g
- Fiber: 4g

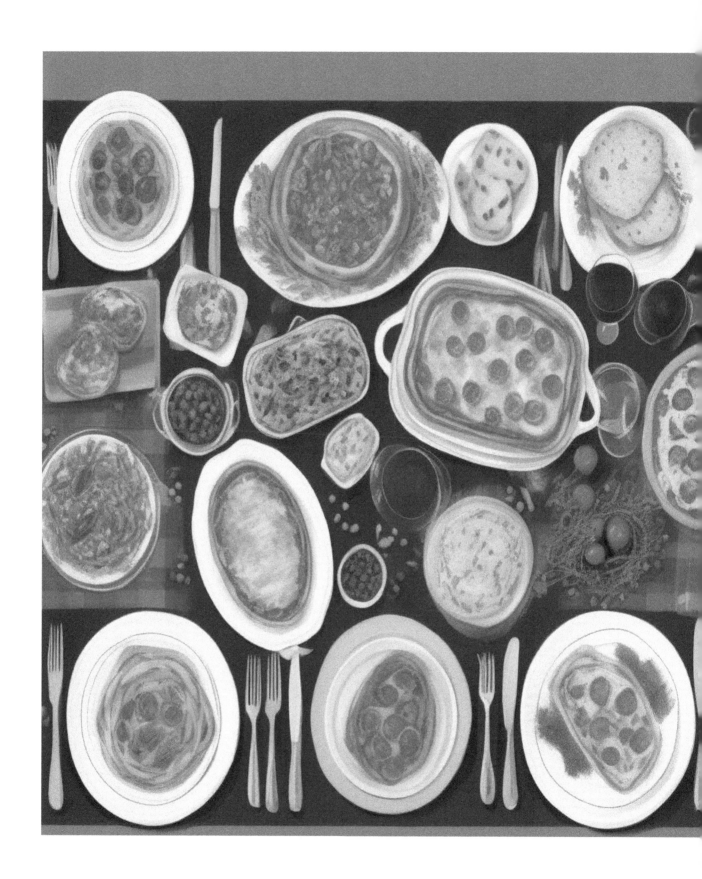

# Chapter 9:Dolci Delights(Desserts)

## CLASSIC TIRAMISU DESSERT

### Ingredients:
- 6 large egg yolks
- 3/4 cup granulated sugar
- 1 cup mascarpone cheese, softened
- 1 1/2 cups strong brewed espresso, cooled
- 1/4 cup coffee liqueur (e.g., Kahlúa)
- 24 to 30 ladyfinger cookies
- Cocoa powder for dusting

### Assembly Instructions:
1. In a heatproof bowl, whisk together egg yolks and sugar. Place the bowl over a pot of simmering water (double boiler) and whisk continuously until the mixture becomes pale and slightly thickened.
2. Remove from heat and let it cool slightly. Add the softened mascarpone cheese and mix until smooth.
3. In a shallow dish, combine the brewed espresso and coffee liqueur.
4. Dip each ladyfinger into the espresso mixture, ensuring they are fully coated but not overly saturated.
5. Arrange a layer of soaked ladyfingers at the bottom of a serving dish.
6. Spread half of the mascarpone mixture over the ladyfingers. Repeat the process for a second layer.
7. Cover and refrigerate the tiramisu for at least 4 hours or overnight.
8. Before serving, dust the top with cocoa powder for a finishing touch.

### Cooking Tips:
- Use room temperature mascarpone for easier blending.

- Adjust the sweetness by modifying the amount of sugar in the egg yolk mixture.


## Nutritional Values (per serving):
- **Calories: 280**
- **Protein: 6g**
- **Fat: 18g**
- **Carbohydrates: 25g**
- **Sugar: 14g**

# CAPRESE SALAD WITH BALSAMIC GLAZE

## Ingredients:
- 4 large ripe tomatoes, sliced
- 1 pound fresh mozzarella cheese, sliced
- Fresh basil leaves
- 1/4 cup extra virgin olive oil
- Balsamic glaze for drizzling
- Salt and pepper to taste

## Assembly Instructions:
1. Arrange alternating slices of tomatoes and mozzarella on a serving platter.
2. Tuck fresh basil leaves between the tomato and mozzarella slices.
3. Drizzle extra virgin olive oil over the salad.
4. Season with salt and pepper to taste.
5. Finish by drizzling balsamic glaze in a crisscross pattern over the salad.

## Cooking Tips:
- Use high-quality, ripe tomatoes for the best flavor.
- Opt for fresh mozzarella for a creamy texture.

## Nutritional Values (per serving):
- Calories: 320
- Protein: 18g
- Fat: 25g
- Carbohydrates: 8g

- Fiber: 2g

These delightful recipes are sure to add a burst of Italian flair to your dining experience, creating a symphony of flavors that capture the essence of this beloved cuisine. Buon Appetito!

# TIRAMISU TRIUMPH

## Ingredients:

- 6 large egg yolks
- 1 cup granulated sugar
- 1 1/4 cups mascarpone cheese
- 1 1/2 cups heavy cream
- 1 cup strong brewed espresso, cooled
- 1/4 cup coffee liqueur (optional)
- 24 to 30 ladyfinger cookies
- Cocoa powder for dusting

## Cooking Instructions:

1. In a large bowl, whisk together egg yolks and sugar until thick and pale. Add mascarpone cheese and mix until smooth.

2. In a separate bowl, whip the heavy cream until stiff peaks form. Gently fold the whipped cream into the mascarpone mixture until well combined.

3. In a shallow dish, combine the brewed espresso and coffee liqueur if using. Dip each ladyfinger into the espresso mixture, ensuring they are evenly soaked but not soggy.

4. In a serving dish, arrange a layer of soaked ladyfingers to cover the bottom. Spread half of the mascarpone mixture over the ladyfingers.

5. Repeat the layers, finishing with a layer of mascarpone mixture on top.

6. Refrigerate the tiramisu for at least 4 hours or preferably overnight to allow the flavors to meld.

7. Before serving, dust the top with cocoa powder for a finishing touch.

## Cooking Tips:

- Use room temperature eggs for easier incorporation into the mascarpone mixture.

- If coffee liqueur is not preferred, you can enhance the espresso with a dash of vanilla extract.

## Nutritional Values:
(Per Serving - Serves 8)
- **Calories: 380**
- **Protein: 6g**
- **Fat: 28g**
- **Carbohydrates: 25g**
- **Fiber: 1g**
- **Sugar: 16g**

# CANNOLI CREATIONS

## Ingredients:

- 2 cups ricotta cheese
- 1 cup powdered sugar
- 1 teaspoon vanilla extract
- 1/2 cup mini chocolate chips
- 12 cannoli shells (store-bought or homemade)
- Powdered sugar for dusting

## Cooking Instructions:

1. In a bowl, combine ricotta cheese, powdered sugar, and vanilla extract. Mix until smooth and creamy.
2. Fold in mini chocolate chips until evenly distributed.
3. Spoon the ricotta mixture into a piping bag and fill each cannoli shell from both ends.
4. Dust the filled cannoli with powdered sugar just before serving.

## Cooking Tips:

- Ensure the ricotta is well-drained to achieve a creamy filling.
- If making cannoli shells at home, fry them until golden brown and crispy.

## Nutritional Values:

(Per Cannoli - Makes 12)
- Calories: 220
- Protein: 5g
- Fat: 12g
- Carbohydrates: 22g
- Fiber: 1g

- Sugar: 12g

# GELATO GALORE

## Ingredients:

- 2 cups whole milk
- 1 cup heavy cream
- 3/4 cup granulated sugar
- 4 large egg yolks
- 1 teaspoon vanilla extract
- Assorted gelato flavors (chocolate, strawberry, pistachio, etc.)

## Cooking Instructions:

1. In a saucepan, heat the milk and cream over medium heat until it begins to simmer. Remove from heat.
2. In a bowl, whisk together sugar and egg yolks until well combined.
3. Gradually pour the hot milk mixture into the egg mixture, whisking constantly.
4. Return the mixture to the saucepan and cook over low heat, stirring constantly until it thickens enough to coat the back of a spoon.
5. Remove from heat, stir in vanilla extract, and let it cool to room temperature.
6. Once cooled, refrigerate the mixture for at least 4 hours or overnight.
7. Churn the custard in an ice cream maker according to the manufacturer's instructions.
8. Layer different gelato flavors in a container, creating a colorful and delicious assortment.

## Cooking Tips:

- Experiment with various gelato flavors to create a vibrant display.

- Allow the gelato to soften slightly before serving for the creamiest texture.

## Nutritional Values:
(Per Serving - Serves 6)
- Calories: 280
- Protein: 5g
- Fat: 20g
- Carbohydrates: 22g
- Fiber: 0g
- Sugar: 20g

# Chapter 10:Beverage Bonanza

## ESPRESSO ELEGANCE

### Ingredients:
- 2 shots of high-quality espresso
- 1 tablespoon of sugar
- 1/4 cup of whole milk
- Cocoa powder for garnish

### Cooking Instructions:
1. Brew two shots of espresso using your preferred method. The richness of the coffee is crucial for the depth of flavor in this recipe.
2. While the espresso is still hot, stir in the sugar until completely dissolved, enhancing the sweetness of the coffee.
3. In a separate pot, heat the milk until it's warm but not boiling. Froth the milk using a steam wand or a handheld frother until it reaches a creamy consistency.
4. Pour the frothed milk over the sweetened espresso, creating a beautiful layer of foam.
5. Optional: Dust the top with cocoa powder for a touch of elegance.
6. Serve immediately and savor the harmonious blend of robust espresso and velvety milk.

### Cooking Tips:
- Use freshly ground coffee beans for the espresso to ensure a bold and aromatic base.
- Experiment with different types of milk for a personalized touch—try almond milk for a nutty flavor or oat milk for creaminess.
- Adjust the sugar quantity to your taste preference, balancing the bitterness of the espresso with sweetness.

## Nutritional Values:
- Serving Size: 1 cup
- Calories: 30
- Protein: 1g
- Fat: 1.5g
- Carbohydrates: 3g

# LIMONCELLO LIBATIONS

## Ingredients:

- 2 ounces of Limoncello liqueur
- 1 ounce of freshly squeezed lemon juice
- 1/2 ounce of simple syrup
- Ice cubes
- Lemon zest for garnish

## Cooking Instructions:

1. Fill a cocktail shaker with ice cubes.
2. Pour in the Limoncello, freshly squeezed lemon juice, and simple syrup.
3. Shake the ingredients vigorously for about 15 seconds to chill the mixture.
4. Strain the liquid into a chilled martini glass or a tumbler filled with ice.
5. Garnish with a twist of lemon zest for a burst of citrus aroma.
6. Enjoy this refreshing Limoncello libation on a warm evening or as a delightful after-dinner drink.

## Cooking Tips:

- For a stronger citrus flavor, infuse the Limoncello with lemon zest for a day before preparing the cocktail.
- Adjust the sweetness by modifying the quantity of simple syrup to suit your taste preferences.

## Nutritional Values:

- Serving Size: 1 cocktail
- Calories: 160
- Carbohydrates: 15g
- Sugars: 14g

# CAPRESE PERFECTION

Ingredients:
- 4 large tomatoes, sliced
- 1 pound fresh mozzarella, sliced
- Fresh basil leaves
- Extra virgin olive oil
- Balsamic glaze
- Salt and black pepper to taste

Assembly Instructions:
1. Arrange tomato and mozzarella slices alternately on a serving platter.
2. Tuck fresh basil leaves between the slices.
3. Drizzle extra virgin olive oil and balsamic glaze over the top.
4. Season with salt and black pepper to taste.
5. Serve immediately as a refreshing antipasto.

Assembly Tips:
- Choose ripe tomatoes and quality fresh mozzarella for the best flavors.
- Adjust the amount of basil to your preference.

Nutritional Values:
(Per Serving - Serves 4)
- Calories: 280
- Protein: 18g
- Fat: 20g
- Carbohydrates: 8g

- Fiber: 2g
- Sugar: 5g

# WINE PAIRING TIPS

## General Guidelines:

- **Red Wines: Pair robust red wines like Chianti or Barolo with hearty Italian dishes such as pasta with rich meat sauces or grilled meats.**
- **White Wines: Lighter white wines like Pinot Grigio or Vermentino complement seafood dishes and lighter pasta sauces.**
- **Sparkling Wines:Prosecco or Asti are excellent choices for appetizers, especially those featuring cured meats and cheeses.**
- **Dessert Wines: Pair sweet dessert wines like Moscato with Italian desserts like tiramisu or cannoli.**

## Specific Recommendations:

- **Espresso Elegance: A shot of grappa or amaro makes a bold and complementary accompaniment to the intense flavors of espresso.**
- **Limoncello Libations:Sip Limoncello on its own as a digestif or pair it with a light and citrusy Italian dessert like lemon sorbet.**

## Wine Pairing Tips:

- **Consider the intensity of flavors in both the dish and the wine to create a harmonious pairing.**
- **Experiment with contrasting or complementary flavors for a dynamic dining experience.**
- **When in doubt, a versatile Chardonnay or Sangiovese can be a safe and enjoyable choice for a wide range of Italian dishes.**

# Chapter 11:Celebration menus

## ROMANTIC DINNERS FOR TWO

Enjoy the enchantment of love with one of our carefully chosen romantic dinners for two. These recipes are meant to fan the flames of desire, whether you're enjoying a peaceful evening or a big occasion. Every dish, from the delicate dance of flavors in our specialty sweets to the velvety richness of our handcrafted pasta, is created to create a culinary symphony that improves the eating experience. Create the ideal atmosphere, light the lights, and allow our recipes to turn your evening into a memorable, passionate meeting.

# FAMILY FEAST EXTRAVAGANZAS

Take your family on a culinary adventure with our family feast extravaganzas, and gather your loved ones around the table. These recipes celebrate family, love, and the pleasure of sharing delicious food—they're more than just a recipe for a dinner. Our meals are designed to unite families across generations, from flavorful roasts that serve as the cornerstone of family traditions to substantial pasta bakes that reflect the coziness of an Italian kitchen. As you serve these hearty feasts, make memories and allow the wine and talk to flow freely. This section pays homage to the essence of Italian cooking, which is the blending of food and family to forge enduring relationships.

# HOLIDAY CELEBRATIONS

**With our assortment of Italian-inspired recipes that give tradition a contemporary spin, you can elevate your holiday celebrations. Whether you're hosting a holiday party for Christmas, New Year's, or any other special event, these recipes are sure to make the occasion genuinely memorable. Every recipe perfectly encapsulates the spirit of the occasion, from lively appetizers that set the mood to jaw-dropping main courses that command attention. Give yourself over to the love of cooking, and allow the fragrances of these meals with Italian influences fill your house with Christmas spirit. It's about making memories of happiness and camaraderie during the most delightful time of the year, not just about the food.**

# QUICK AND EASY WEEKNIGHT MEALS

A tasty, home-cooked dinner shouldn't have to be sacrificed because of a hectic schedule. Explore our selection of simple and quick evening dishes that will expedite your cooking without sacrificing quality. These recipes, which range from tasty one-pan meals to quick pasta dishes, are ideal for busy evenings when time is of the importance. Learn the secret to quick, delicious cooking so that every weekday can be a stress-free culinary adventure.

## Healthy and Vibrant Italian Fare

With our assortment of nutritious and flavorful Italian cuisine, you may satisfy your palate and nourish your body. Examine dishes that highlight the nutrient-dense aspect of Italian cooking without sacrificing flavor. These recipes provide a well-rounded way to savor the tastes of Italy, from vibrant salads brimming with fresh vegetables to light yet filling seafood entrees. Accept the Mediterranean way of life by consuming foods that improve your general health in addition to tasting excellent. Discover the wonderful and heart-healthy world of Italian cooking, demonstrating that filling meals can be both healthful and decadent.

# Chapter 12: Tips for mastering Italian cuisine

## FLAVOR BALANCING:

Mastering the art of Italian food involves striking the ideal balance of flavors, and Chapter 12.1 will walk you through the process of becoming a culinary symphony. We examine the complex ballet of flavors that characterizes Italian cuisine, from the strong undertones of garlic and olive oil to the subtle harmony of fresh herbs. Learn how to play with opposing textures to create a sensory experience that will take your cuisine to new heights and the secrets of striking the perfect balance between acidity and sweetness. This section provides you with useful advice and ideas to help you add the complex, well-balanced flavors that define real Italian cuisine to your creations.

# Menu Planning:

Any food aficionado should know how to create a well-balanced and enjoyable menu, and Chapter 12.2 is your guide when it comes to Italian menu planning. Explore the skill of pairing food to create a flow that transports customers' palates through a variety of flavors and textures. Learn the fundamentals of creating an Italian menu that highlights the variety of the cuisine, from antipasti to dolci. This section offers helpful tips to make sure your menu is more than just a selection of foods; rather, it's a carefully thought-out experience that will stay in the minds of your guests, whether you're hosting a joyful gathering or a casual family meal.

# Culinary Troubleshooting:

In the kitchen, even the most experienced chefs have difficulties. Chapter 12.3 will help you navigate the waters of culinary troubleshooting. This section provides useful remedies to common culinary problems, such as fixing overdone pasta or salvaging an ill-advised sauce. Gain the confidence to use culinary errors as chances for creativity by mastering the art of improvisation. With troubleshooting methods and ideas at your disposal, you'll be able to handle any kitchen emergency with ease and be prepared to serve faultless Italian dishes that showcase your tenacity and love for the cuisine. When it comes to cooking, every obstacle is an opportunity to improve your abilities and turn every dish into a success.

## Wine Pairing:

The ideal wine matching completes any Italian dining experience and reveals the techniques for balancing the tastes of your food with the best Italian wines. Learn how to choose wines that complement and enrich a meal, from the robust reds of Chianti to the bubbly fizz of Prosecco. To ensure that every sip accentuates the subtleties of your expertly produced Italian creations, this section walks you through the fundamentals of harmonizing acidity, tannins, and sweetness. Discover the delights of the ideal combination to enhance your eating experiences, regardless of your level of wine expertise.

## Seasonal Sensations:

Recognize the abundance of every season, from the colorful spring veggies to the filling winter root vegetables. This part takes you on a tour of the market booths to help you choose the freshest produce and skillfully incorporate it into your meals. Learn to love cooking in accordance with the changing of the seasons, allowing each ingredient's inherent flavor to come through, and produce meals that capture the spirit of Italy all year long.

Enter these chapters, where wine pairing, seasonal delights, meal planning, troubleshooting, and flavor balancing come together to make your kitchen an Italian culinary paradise. May you find inspiration, ardor, and the delight of experiencing the true flavors of Italy as you peruse these pages.

# Conculsion

As I bring this culinary journey to a close, "Italian Mastery: A Culinary Journey 2024," I would want to express my sincere gratitude for joining me on this tasty journey. Together, we have explored the many facets of Italy's culinary history, learning the trade secrets, methods, and anecdotes that make Italian cooking a timeless art form. When you turn the last page of this cookbook, think of it as more than just a recipe book—rather, see it as an all-encompassing manual—a reliable ally in your quest for Italian culinary expertise.

I hope the chapters in this exploration have deepened your grasp of the subtleties that characterize this excellent dining. Our journey started with the goal of improving your Italian mastery techniques. From creating thoughtful menus to mastering the art of wine pairing, from solving kitchen obstacles to perfecting the delicate balance of flavors, every component has been painstakingly crafted to provide you with the knowledge and confidence required to produce authentic Italian cuisine.

As you venture forth into your kitchen, armed with newfound skills and a palate tuned to the subtleties of Italian flavors, I encourage you to embrace the joy of experimentation. Let your creativity flow, and don't be afraid to add your personal touch to the traditional recipes shared within these pages. After all, the heart of Italian cooking lies not just in adherence to tradition but in the spirit of innovation and love that you infuse into every dish.

Remember that the journey doesn't end here; it merely transforms. The recipes, tips, and techniques presented in this book are the foundation upon which you can build a lifetime of culinary exploration. Share the joy of cooking with family and friends, creating moments that transcend the dining table and become cherished memories.

As you savor the fruits of your labor, may the aromas, flavors, and textures transport you to the enchanting streets of Italy. Whether you're recreating a classic dish or experimenting with a new creation, may the spirit of Italian cuisine infuse every moment with delight and satisfaction.

# GLOSSARY OF TERMS

**Aromatics:**

Ingredients such as garlic, onions, and herbs that contribute aromatic flavors to dishes.

**Al Dente:**

Italian for "to the tooth," referring to pasta that is cooked firm when bitten.

**Béchamel:**

A classic white sauce made from butter, flour, and milk, often used in Italian lasagna.

**Bruschetta:**

Toasted bread rubbed with garlic, topped with diced tomatoes, fresh basil, and drizzled with olive oil.

**Caponata:**

A Sicilian eggplant dish consisting of diced vegetables, olives, and capers in a sweet and sour sauce.

**Carnaroli Rice:**

A premium Italian rice variety commonly used in risotto for its firm texture and ability to absorb flavors.

**Cacciatore:**

A dish, often chicken, cooked with tomatoes, onions, mushrooms, and herbs, meaning "hunter" in Italian.

## Dolci:

Italian for desserts, encompassing a variety of sweet treats like tiramisu, cannoli, and panna cotta.

## Frittata:

An Italian omelet made with eggs and various ingredients like vegetables, cheese, or meats.

## Gelato:

Italian ice cream known for its dense and creamy texture, made with a higher proportion of milk to cream.

## Mirepoix:

A mixture of diced onions, carrots, and celery, used as a flavor base in Italian sauces and soups.

## Orecchiette:

Small, ear-shaped pasta often used in Southern Italian dishes, particularly in Puglia.

## Pesto:

A sauce made from basil, garlic, pine nuts, Parmesan cheese, and olive oil, typically used with pasta.

## Ragu:

A slow-cooked meat sauce, commonly made with ground beef or pork, tomatoes, and aromatic seasonings.

## Semolina:

Coarsely ground durum wheat used to make pasta and other Italian baked goods.

## Tiramisu:
A popular Italian dessert made with layers of coffee-soaked ladyfingers and mascarpone cheese.

## Vongole:
Italian for clams, often used to prepare dishes like Linguine alle Vongole, a pasta with clam sauce.

## Zabaione:
A light custard dessert made with egg yolks, sugar, and sweet wine, often Marsala.

This glossary is designed to enhance your understanding of key Italian culinary terms as you embark on your journey of mastering the art of Italian cooking.

# ABOUT THE AUTHOR:

I am thrilled to welcome you to the culinary journey that is "Italian Mastery: A Culinary Journey 2024." As the author, my name is Katherine W McCurley, and I am passionate about sharing the secrets and joys of Italian cooking with you.

My love affair with Italian cuisine began during a trip to the picturesque streets of Florence, where the aroma of freshly baked focaccia and the melodies of bustling markets ignited a passion that would shape my culinary endeavors. Over the years, I have immersed myself in the diverse regional flavors of Italy, learning from local chefs, exploring markets, and mastering the art of crafting authentic dishes.

In "Italian Mastery," I aim to be your guide, sharing not just recipes but the techniques, insights, and strategies that will elevate your Italian mastering strategies. Each page is infused with my commitment to authenticity and a genuine desire to make your culinary experience as delightful and rewarding as possible.

Whether you're a seasoned chef or a kitchen novice, my hope is that this book becomes a companion in your culinary adventures, empowering you to create Italian dishes that bring joy and satisfaction to your table. May your kitchen be filled with the warmth of Italian flavors, and may each recipe be a step towards mastering the art of Italian cuisine.

*Katherine W McCurley*

www.ingramcontent.com/pod-product-compliance
Ingram Content Group UK Ltd.
Pitfield, Milton Keynes, MK11 3LW, UK
UKHW051412201224
3801UKWH00053B/1825